Bears are big, **BIG** animals.

MW01026716

Polar bears are among the biggest of all.

Grizzly bears are nearly as big as polar bears.

Black bears and giant pandas are a little smaller.

Big bears have long, strong claws.
The grizzly's claws help it to catch fish.

Black bears use their claws
to help them climb trees.

Polar bears use their claws to grip the slippery ice.

The giant panda has five claws *plus* a thumb to help the panda hold its favorite food – bamboo.

Most bears spend the winter asleep in dry, safe caves or dens.

Baby bears, called cubs, are born during the winter. They snuggle against their mother to keep warm.

By spring the cubs are ready to go outside. They explore and play.

The mother bear cuddles and
feeds her cubs.

Bears eat and eat and eat during the spring and summer. They nibble plants and berries . . .

and catch delicious pink salmon.

By fall the bear cubs have grown bigger.

Now they must look for a warm den
in which to spend . . .

the cold, cold days of winter.